The Effect of Heat Upon Clays

Albert Bleininger

The Effect of Heat Upon Clays

BY

PROF. A. V. BLEININGER, B. Sc.

Director of Ceramic Department of University
of Illinois.

T. A. RANDALL & CO.
Publishers,
Indianapolis, Ind.

PREFACE

"The Effect of Heat Upon Clays" is a subject of vital interest to every clayworker. 'Tis said there are no two clays alike. Each clay has properties peculiar to itself, hence to insure the best results in product and economy in manufacture, each clay must be studied carefully and treated in a manner best adapted to develop the highest grade of ware, whether it be brick, tile or pottery, at the lowest cost. With a view of aiding clayworkers to solve some of the many difficult problems incident to the variation in clays, Prof. A. V. Bleininger some years ago prepared a treatise on this subject for THE CLAY-WORKER, which was published in serial form. The subject is of such prime importance that the matter has been revised by the author and is now presented in book form for library and reference purposes.

TABLE OF CONTENTS.

CHAPTER IV.

CHAPTER V.

CHAPTER VI.

THE EFFECT OF HEAT UPON CLAYS.

By A. V. Bleininger.

CHAPTER I.—CONSTITUENTS OF CLAY.

THE FINAL VALUE of clay products depends upon the success with which the operation of burning has been carried out. Burning changes the raw clay into a hard, stone like material, useful in many forms. The heat applied in our kilns does work upon the clay just as it does work in converting water into steam to be transformed into power in the steam engine. This work is partly chemical and partly physical.

In order that we may be able to study the effect of heat upon clay, it becomes necessary that first of all we examine its make-up, just as it is necessary to know the structure of a machine or apparatus before we can speak intelligently about the operation of the same. Without going into a lengthy geological discussion of the origin of clay with which we meet so often, at almost every convention of clayworkers and in every clay report, we shall now examine briefly the mineral constituents of all clays, for it must be remembered that clays are complex rocks made up of a considerable number of minerals, each of which contributes its share to the total character of a certain material.

An examination of the anatomy of a clay reveals the following constituents:

1. Clay substance.
2. Quartz.
3. Feldspar.
4. Mica.
5. Iron compounds.
   a. Ferric oxide.
   b. Ferrous oxide.
   c. Ferrous carbonate.
   d. Ferrous sulphide.
   e. Ferrous silicate.
6. Lime compounds.
   a. Lime carbonate.
   b. Lime sulphate.
7. Sulphur.
   a. Sulphides.
   b. Sulphates.
8. Carbon.
   a. Vegetable matter.
   b. Bituminous.
   c. Fixed carbon.
9. Gases.
   a. Water.
   b. Carbonic acid gas.
   c. Sulphurous acid.
   d. Sulphuric acid.

1. **Clay Substance.** By this we mean that part of clay which gives it its real plasticity; that is, the ability to be shaped and molded. The purest kind is called kaolinite, which is a white clay, composed practically of 46 per cent. of silica, 39 per cent of alumina, and 14 per cent. of chemical water; in other words, it is a hydrous silicate of alumina. This substance occurs in many variations, more or less pure and more or less plastic. The purest kind is not usually the most plastic, since pure white kaolins frequently possess but little plasticity, form a weak, dusty body on drying, and burn to a more or less porous mass. On the other hand, the more impure clay substance, such as ball clay, is tough and plastic, becomes hornlike when drying and burns to a dense body at quite low temperatures. The difference between the two kinds of clay substances in regard to color is, however, in favor of the kaolin, which produces a pure white color on burning, while the ball clay assumes more or less of a yellowish shade. This is the reason why potters must have as much kaolin in their clay compositions as possible, consistent with the working quality required.

All clays, whatever they may be used for, contain more or less of this clay substance in various stages of purity. It is this part of the clay composition which causes shrinkage in drying and burning, and which sometimes gives trouble in drying. In itself clay substance is very refractory and withstands very high temperatures. The water which was observed to be a part of the composition of clay is not ordinary free water, but is in a state of combination and hence is called chemical water. It does not evaporate like water ordinarily does, but remains in the clay as part of its solid structure, and only escapes as steam when the temperature of 600 degrees C. is reached.

2. **Quartz.** This mineral occurring in clays as fine or coarse sand consists practically entirely of silica. It is a hard, non-plastic material, quite refractory, but not nearly as much so as pure clay substance. A pure clay fire brick hence excels a silica fire brick as well as bricks made from a silicious clay in resisting heat.

The quartz may thus be said to constitute a large part of the sandy matter of clays. Owing to its non-plastic quality, it will, when mixed with clay, decrease the drying shrinkage. A certain amount of quartz is useful for not only this purpose, but is also necessary to promote the chemical union between the various constituents of clay in the process of vitrification. It must be understood, however, that for this last purpose it must be quite fine and not excessive in amount; a condition most frequently met with in shales, and less so in the alluvial clays. Coarser sand particles are practically of no value for chemical combination, and again, too large an amount of fine quartz will either result in too glassy and brittle a body or it will cause very serious defects, which are due to a very curious property of quartz. This mineral, when heated up to a red heat, is found to expand in volume in a rather erratic manner; this expansion being quite large in amount as well as irregular. The result is, that if the amount of quartz is large the clay will suffer expansion in place of contraction in the kiln. It is told of one man, not knowing this peculiar property of quartz or sand, that he used a very sandy clay in making bricks which he set quite high in the kiln. The result was that the arch was actually lifted up by the expansion of the bricks.

Even though this peculiar behavior of quartz is not shown by the apparent expansion of the brick, it may cause the structure of the burnt clay to be "rotten," resulting in ware which does not ring, but sounds dead and has poor strength and wearing quality.

3. **Feldspar.** This mineral also is present in every clay. The chemical composition of a typical feldspar, called orthoclase, is 67.4 per cent. of silica, 18.4 per cent. of alumina, and 16.9 per cent. of potash. This mineral constituent, unlike clay substance and quartz, is not refractory, but melts at about 1,200 degrees C. It is, hence, a flux, and when present in a clay, causes the latter to vitrify and finally to melt at a far lower temperature than applies to clay substance or quartz alone. This is the reason why potters add feldspar to their pottery mixtures in order to obtain vitrified wares. Another peculiar fact is, that when feldspar is mixed with quartz, in about the proportion of 75 per cent. feldspar and 25 per cent. quartz, this mixture again vitrifies and melts at a lower temperature than feldspar alone.

One rather beneficial feature of the fluxing of feldspar is that its action is quite slow, and hence it does not cause vitrification to take place so rapidly that trouble may ensue if a kiln happens to be somewhat overfired, as is true of some other fluxes. Feldspar may be considered therefore as a safe flux.

4. **Mica.** This mineral occurs in clay in smaller or larger amounts in the shape of very thin flakes, corresponding to the mica used in stoves. These flakes of mica have the distinctive peculiarity of being capable of splitting up into an infinite number of very thin flakes, just as may be observed in the large sheets of mica used for various purposes. This flakey character of mica in clay makes it difficult to separate it from the light clay substance and also in grinding a clay

it is almost impossible to reduce the size of the mica particles, which are very elusive and slip through between the grinding surfaces without suffering much damage. Mica, like action, and this is emphasized still more by the fact that only the dust-like particles really assist in the fluxing action. The large flakes contribute but little in this respect. Unlike feld-feldspar, is a flux, but is much weaker than the latter in its spar, mica does not burn to a white color, but results in a dark or reddish color. This explains why some kaolins containing mica, though apparently white in the raw state, will burn to a dark color.

Such kaolins are unfit for pottery making since it is practically impossible to float off the mica plates by washing. The dark color of the mica is due to iron content.

These four minerals thus constitute the main body of many clays, and in burning the resulting burnt body is the product of the joint action of these constituents. The constituents predominating in amount will, of course, impart to the clay its prominent features.

5. **Iron Compounds.** While the pure white burning clays contain but little iron, the amount of this element becomes greater and greater as the clay is found to burn buff or red. It might be said right here that iron in its various forms is a powerful flux. Two prominent forms of iron are its two oxides, ferric and ferrous oxide. In the pure state, ferric oxide, a combination of 112 parts, by weight, of iron, and 48 parts, by weight, of oxygen, is of a red color, as is shown by many iron ores, also by red ochre or red clays, both of which contain iron in this combination. It may be prepared artificially by pouring nitric acid over iron filings and dissolving them. On boiling down this acid liquid, crystals will be ob-

tained, and when these are heated to a red heat there will be left behind a red powder, which is ferric oxide. Red building bricks contain their iron in the form of this oxide. Though a flux, ferric oxide is not violent in its action, but is rather slow in promoting vitrification, and hence is safe, not being liable to cause vitrification or fusion to take place so rapidly as to do harm.

Ferrous oxide, on the other hand, consists of 112 parts, by weight, of iron, and 32 parts, by weight, of oxygen, containing thus less oxygen than the ferric form by 16 parts. Its typical form is illustrated by blacksmith's scales, which, as we know, are black in color. There is hence a distinct color distinction between the ferric and ferrous oxides. But this is not the only distinction. Ferrous oxide is a violent flux, combining with the silica of clay rapidly and forming a ferrous silicate which is dark in color. This compound is illustrated by the slag of the open hearth furnace, which is quite fusible and black.

Now this difference between the two oxides is brought out very strikingly by red and black bricks. The red brick evidently contains the ferric oxide, the black paving brick ferrous oxide, combined with the silica as ferrous silicate.

We have noted that the difference between the two oxides is only that the ferric form contains more oxygen than the ferrous. This extra oxygen is expelled when the furnace conditions are reducing; that is, when the kiln space is filled with gases which are partially unburnt. These hot combustible gases are very eager for oxygen, and hence deprive the red, ferric oxide of its loose part of oxygen, changing it to the black ferrous oxide. If immediately after this exchange of oxygen we again admit plenty of air into the kiln it is possible to convert the black oxide back to the red. In fact, this takes place constantly in our kilns, so that in spite of occasionally heavy firing, which corresponds to reduction, we finally finish the burn with resulting red brick. However, on maintaining the reducing fire longer, during the high temperature stage of burning, the resulting ferrous oxide which we know is eager to combine with silica, actually enters into this union, forming a ferrous silicate which no longer oxidizes readily, and hence stays black. In other words, when this reaction takes place we no longer have the iron in the loose condition, but in a state where it is firmly bound to the silica, and hence is not so susceptible to the influence of the oxygen of the air.

The practical result then must be black or at least dark colored brick, and the stronger the reducing action, that is, the heavier we have fired, the darker must this color be, depending, of course, also upon the iron content of the clay, for if there is but little iron present there is evidently but slight chance for reduction. Let us keep the distinction between ferric and ferrous oxide clearly in mind.

Beside the two oxides of iron we may have iron present in other forms, as will be shown presently.

Ferrous Carbonate. This compound may be assumed to be composed of 72 parts, by weight, of ferrous oxide, and 44 parts of carbon dioxide or carbonic acid, as this compound is commonly called, which is really gaseous. If we heat ferrous carbonate the gas goes off and leaves ferrous oxide, which behaves as if it had always been this oxide. The driving off of the carbonic acid is exactly the same thing that happens when limestone is burnt. There, as we know, great quantities of carbonic acid are expelled, leaving quicklime, as the chemists call it, calcium oxide.

For all practical purposes, therefore, the ferrous carbonate is not a bit different from ferrous oxide, for the latter is invariably left behind, since the gas escapes.

Ferrous Sulphide. Often on examining a clay we find small crystals or grains of a mineral resembling gold, which goes by the popular name of fool's gold. Its real name is iron pyrites, and it is composed of 56 parts of iron and 64 parts of sulphur; it is ferrous sulphide. These crystals may be so small that we do not catch the glistening, gold-like effect. We see from its composition that ferrous sulphide contains no oxygen in its make-up, and hence we can not say that ferrous oxide is a part of it. But let us look into the matter and observe what happens to the iron pyrite on heating it in a kiln. We will find that the sulphur burns out and leaves as a gas, sulphur dioxide, and at the same time 16 parts, by weight, of oxygen are taken from the air in the kiln and combine with the 56 parts of iron left behind after getting rid of the sulphur. We have again, then, 56 parts of iron plus 16 parts of oxygen, which is equal to 72 parts of ferrous oxide. Here, too, we finish with having ferrous oxide, which, of course, acts according to its nature.

Ferrous Silicate. Nature furnishes us in clay also some ferrous oxide already combined with silica, but this kind of material is comparatively small in amount. Since in ferrous silicate the iron oxide is already combined, reducing gases do not affect it. In the mineral augite, hornblende and others, we have examples of this kind of iron compound. As the clay vitrifies these minerals gradually fuse and merge with the other compounds of the clay which are present in larger quantities.

In taking finely ground sand, mixing it intimately with

ferric oxide, and burning it in a kiln in which a reducing fire is maintained, we shall find a ferrous silicate produced. Similarly, we find contained in clay some natural silicates which are, in part, at least, ferrous silicates, and which would thus tend to impart to the clays a dark color. In some clays the quantity of such minerals present is considerable, and we would be compelled to burn them very carefully, indeed, if we wanted to produce a good, red color. Fortunately, however, most clays contain comparatively small amounts of unchanged ferrous silicate minerals, and hence we are usually able to carry out the oxidization of the iron in the clay without trouble as far as this constituent is concerned. Some common minerals of this type are hornblende, augite, and mica. Though, perhaps, it is practically impossible to observe them in a clay without the aid of a microscope, their acquaintance can be made by observing the structure of the granite boulders which are scattered plentifully throughout our Northern States. The black or brown crystals noted on the surface of such a granite are mostly representatives of the families represented by the above three minerals. Since, then, the clays are derived from just such rocks as granite, it may easily be understood how the ferrous silicates got into the clay. In no case is the reaction of the combined iron in the clay so sudden as in the case of the free ferrous oxide, and hence not so disastrous. While the free oxide may combine with its quota of silica so quickly that the ware is softened and often distorted so as to ruin the value of the product, the combined oxide in the silicate promotes vitrification more leisurely.

Lime Compounds. Nearly all clays contain greater or smaller quantities of lime, and there are two principal forms of the latter, the more important of which is lime carbonate.

Chemically, the carbonate is composed of two substances, a solid which we know as caustic lime, and a gas, commonly called carbonic acid. Lime carbonate we know well in the shape of limestone, marl, marble, etc., and owing to its great quantity in nature it is not surprising that it appears in clays. In many clays it is detected by simply pouring a little muriatic acid on a lump of the material. The presence of the carbonate is at once indicated by the effervescence caused by the escape of the carbonic acid gas, which is displaced by the stronger acid. The more lime the clay contains, the more lively will be the sizzling thus caused, it being often like the noise made by a miniature soda fountain. Now let us examine the action of the lime carbonate upon clays. As long as the carbonic acid remains combined with the caustic lime, or calcium oxide, as the chemists call it, no reaction will take place. However, when the heat is raised in a kiln, to about 900 degrees C., the gas is forced to leave, and there remains behind the quick lime. This at once begins to unite and react with the clay, and if enough of the lime is present and the heat is raised, the clay will vitrify and soon melt down to a slag. The peculiar part of this reaction is its suddenness. There is little time allowed between the vitrification and fusion, and unless the burner is skillful, and the kiln well designed, trouble is bound to come. The writer has frequently observed that the time interval between the proper burning of the ware and fusion was not more than thirty minutes. That this makes it difficult, if not impossible, to burn vitrified products from such a clay goes without saying, though, of course, it is possible to produce ware which need not be vitrified. Even in this case, considerable care must be exercised. Another peculiarity of such clays is that the color of the brick, etc., is changed from red to buff, by virtue of some reaction of the lime with any iron oxide present in the clay. This can easily be proven by taking some of the clay from which the buff Milwaukee bricks are made, extracting nearly all of the lime carbonate by treatment with dilute muriatic acid, and burning the clay. It will be found to burn red, showing clearly that the clay does not contain sufficient iron to cause it to burn red, but that the lime caused the change to the buff color.

Another effect of the lime is to be observed when the carbonate is present in the clay not in a state of fine subdivision, as has been tacitly assumed so far, but in the shape of nodules or grains of larger or smaller size. These particles undergo the same decomposition on heating, but the resulting quicklime, owing to its occurrence in larger grains, can not unite with the clay completely, in fact, only at the surface. The interior of the nodules still remains quicklime. The consequences are evident. As soon as the brick is used or becomes moist the quicklime slakes. But the slaking of lime always means that it gets larger in volume, and if restrained, it is able to exert a powerful force which, in the case of the brick, means the destruction of the latter. In dealing with clays containing lime we are, hence, confronted by two possible methods of dealing with them. Either the lime nodules can be removed from the clay by means of some kind of a separator, or by washing, or the clay must be ground so fine that all of the lime grains are reduced to a state of division insuring its complete union and combination with the clay proper. Where the lime grains are too fine for separation by machinery the first process, of course, can not be adopted. In either case the process adopted must be followed strictly, and no intermediate method can produce good ware. Insufficient separation will cause bad ware just as poor grinding would do. Wherever the lime carbonate occurs in fairly large nodules or "lime kidneys," the cheaper way would certainly be the separation process.

Beside the carbonate we have another lime compound in clay. and this is the sulphate of lime. As the name implies, it is a combination of quicklime and sulphuric acid, just as the carbonate consisted of quicklime and carbonic acid. The sulphuric acid is much more powerful, chemically, than the carbonic acid, hence it is not so easily expelled from its union with lime. In fact, the breaking apart of the sulphate of lime does not take place except at quite high temperatures, which are beyond the reach of the red brick manufacturer. The result is evidently that the lime present as the sulphate does not bring about such a rapid vitrification and fusion as is observed with the carbonate, unless we employ some powerful agents for expelling the sulphuric acid. The latter, like the carbonic acid, is gaseous at the temperature of the brick kilns. The manufacturer of hard porcelain can use lime sulphate as a flux, because he employs a temperature greatly in excess of the heat a red brick is able to resist, and also because he can cause heavy smoke to pass through his kiln without injury to the ware, a procedure which hastens the dissociation of the sulphate to a great extent. This being the case, we can understand that clays containing iron oxide and lime sulphate in place of lime carbonate will not produce a buff color, but will remain red burning.

The lime sulphate may be originally contained in clay, as such, in the form of gypsum crystals, which are white, transparent and soft, and of all sizes, from the beautiful, well-defined specimen to the extremely fine grains which are almost invisible to the naked eye. Often we may find very little gypsum in the clay, though considerable lime may be present as the carbonate Yet after burning, considerable lime sulphate may be found present. The question thus arises: Whence came this sulphate? The question is usually answered by examining the coal used. It will be found to contain sulphur in the form of iron pyrites. As we know, the sulphur of this compound burns to sulphurous acid, and this, during the earlier stages of the burn, is changed to sulphuric acid. On passing through the kiln this sulphuric acid gas finds an easy victim in the carbonate of lime. The carbonic acid is compelled to leave, and the sulphuric acid takes possession of the lime. This is the same action which would happen if we were to pour sulphuric acid out of a bottle upon limestone, that is, sulphate of lime is formed. Similarly, when a clay contains pyrites and carbonate of lime, the same thing will happen, resulting in the formation of sulphuric acid.

Sulphur. Any one doubting the existence of sulphur in clay need only observe the white vapor arising from the stacks of most brick kilns, or, still better, test the odor of their fumes. They will be found to be stifling, with the characteristic smell if burning sulphur. At one shale-brick plant, with which the writer is acquainted, the quantity of sulphur escaping daily in the shape of sulphuric acid is about 3.6 tons, and the stack of the continuous kiln is constantly plumed with a cloud of white vapor. It is safe to say that the greatest part of this sulphuric acid vapor has come from the iron pyrites contained either in the clay or the coal, or both. The formation of this vapor is, hence, due to the burning of the sulphur, which is part of the pyrites, forming sulphurous acid. This, as it passes through the moist atmosphere of the kiln, will form the sulphuric acid. The pyrites are decomposed at about the time the chemical water is expelled, and hence then we will find the maximum amount of sulphuric acid present. As the heat rises, less and less of the sulphuric acid gas will be found in the fire gases, until finally but little sulphuric acid is evolved, owing to the fact that, of course, the amount of iron sulphide in the clay constantly becomes smaller, and also that after the expulsion of the chemical water of the clay most of the sulphur, whether coming from the clay or the coal, leaves as sulphurous acid, whose chemical activity is far less powerful than that of its relation. While the anhydrous sulphuric acid contains 32 parts of sulphur and 48 parts of oxygen, the sulphurous acid gas is composed of 32 parts of sulphur and 32 parts of oxygen. The sulphuric acid gas is extremely corrosive in its action, and has a most suffocating odor, while the sulphurous acid gas is lighter and has exactly the odor of burning sulphur, which, though pungent, is not as extremely suffocating as is the vapor of the more active compound.

In the presence of considerable sulphate of lime, and when the burning is carried on either at a very high temperature or with strongly reducing firing conditions at a lower temperature, the lime sulphate is decomposed into quicklime, which at once combines with the clay and sulphurous acid gas. As has already been indicated, the sulphurous acid can not form sulphuric acid at the higher temperatures, and hence escapes unchanged. The observant reader might wonder how the lime sulphate, which is a combination of quicklime and sulphuric acid, could be made to yield quicklime and sulphurous acid. This is due to the fact that carbon from the unburnt fire gases is a most potent agent in reducing even a strong compound like sulphuric acid to its lower stages, and it is only due to the fact that the sulphuric acid is reduced to sulphurous that it may be expelled. Without this reduction, that is, as sulphuric acid, it could not be caused to leave.

Carbon. This ever-present constituent of clays plays an important role in the burning process. It can easily be shown that carbon is to be found in practically every clay, though, of course, the amount varies from large percentages down to slight quantities. Some shales, for instance, on being brought in contact with a flame, seem to burn almost like coal, and when distilled give off large volumes of combustible gases. It is also quite apparent that the kind of carbon found in clays must differ quite considerably. In the soft clays close to the soil we should expect to find carbon in the shape of vegetable matter, roots, etc.; in the black shales we meet carbon in the form of bituminous matter, which resembles tar or asphalt, and again, in some shales, once subjected to great rock pressure, we observe the carbon in a form resembling anthracite, or even graphite. It is quite evident that each kind of carbon, when caused to be consumed in the kiln, will burn differently, just as petroleum burns differently from bituminous or anthracite coal. The main difference lies between the volatile and the non-volatile carbon compounds. The former, evidently as soon as the heat is raised, will distill out of the clay and burn on the surface on contact with the air. The fixed carbon will remain within the clay body and will be burnt when the opportunity is offered for the entrance of air. It also becomes obvious that the density of the clay in which the carbon is incorporated has a great deal to do with the rapidity of burning. The carbon can not burn any faster than air is supplied to it, and air can filter through a fine-grained clay but very slowly. This means that in order to burn all of the carbon completely we must allow air at a low temperature to surround the ware for some time. It is necessary to maintain a low temperature, since raising the heat would tend to make the clay still more dense, so that but very little carbon could burn, and the result would be that a good deal of the latter would remain in the clay.

Just how difficult it is to burn carbon contained in clay may be illustrated by a simple experiment. Take some coal, either pulverized or in lumps, and incorporate it in clay. Dry and burn the latter. It will be observed that it is not an easy matter to accomplish this without some injurious effects on the clay, and this is still more true when the clay is molded under pressure, as is the case with dry-pressed or stiff-clay brick.

Some one might now ask why it is necessary to burn out the carbon at all, why not leave it in the clay and go on with the burning? That this will not do has been frequently demonstrated, and most thoroughly so by the exhaustive work of Professor Orton. A variety of troubles are liable to arise in this connection, to some of which attention is called briefly. As the reader will remember, the iron of the clay is present in two states, the ferric and the ferrous oxides. Since the ferric oxide contains some oxygen which it can spare, the latter is appropriated by the carbon in the clay, owing to the fact that carbon has a powerful tendency to oxidize, that is, to burn. Consequently all of the iron of the clay, in the presence of carbon, will remain as the ferrous oxide. This, as we know, combines greedily with the silica of the clay, and results in the formation of a readily fusible ferrous silicate. The brick, hence, vitrifies around the core still containing the carbon, and tends to enclose it in a dense matrix. But some of the carbon, be it ever so little, continues to burn and to form either of the gases, carbon monoxide or carbon dioxide. Since these find their way outward blocked either entirely or in part, they will exert a pressure which will distend or bloat the brick. Of course this practically destroys the structure of the ware for any useful purpose. It is quite evident, therefore, that the clay must be thoroughly oxidized by being kept bathed in an atmosphere of air at a moderate temperature until all of the carbon has been burnt out. This feature will be discussed more fully when we come to speak of the burning process.

Gases. As we have already seen, there is no lack of gases formed in clay. The principal ones are steam from the pore and chemical water, carbonic acid gas from the carbonate of lime, the ferrous carbonate and the burning of the carbon; sulphurous acid from the burning of the pyrite, and sulphuric acid gas from the pyrites and the decomposition of sulphates. That ample opportunity must be given these to escape is obvious, and our burning operations must be conducted accordingly. In addition we must deal with the chemical action of the sulphurous and sulphuric acid gases which, as we know, are powerful chemical agents. Also, at times we have considerable volumes of oxygen given off from the clay.

We are now ready to discuss the burning process itself, and its effects upon the reactions taking place within the clay. For this purpose we can divide the burning into four periods:

1. Watersmoking.
2. Dehydration.
3. Oxidization.
4. Vitrification.

CHAPTER II.

Watersmoking.

WHEN WE FIRST begin to fire a kiln of clayware the heat, as all clayworkers know, is raised very slowly and gradually, and the temperature is quite low, not more than 200 degrees Centigrade. The main object of this procedure is, of course, to expel the water remaining in the ware. Though the bricks may come from the dryer in the bone-dry condition, they still contain water which we call hygroscopic water. This water differs from the water which leaves the clay in drying in being difficult to drive off. It seems to cling tenaciously to the particles of clay and requires much more heat for its expulsion. Clay seems to have a great absorbing power for moisture, and in fact many other gases. In taking clay which has been watersmoked, that is, clay really dry, and exposing it to the air, it will be found to gain in weight rapidly. This is due to the fact that water vapor from the air has been absorbed. Similarly, other gases like ammonia are taken up in large volumes. Clay thus behaves similarly to charcoal as to this peculiar absorbing power, a fact already recognized by the ancients.

Although this hygroscopic water requires a higher temperature for its expulsion, care must yet be taken that the temperature is not carried up too high. If the thermometer registers too high a temperature the heat penetrates into the brick too rapidly and too much of the hygroscopic water flashes into steam. This is disastrous for there is only limited room within the pore space of the bricks. A brick of, say, 100 cubic inches volume and 20 per cent. pore space can not hold safely more than twenty cubic inches of steam. If we raise the heat not only is more water evaporated from the inside of the brick, but the steam also expands, and consequently pressure is exerted upon the pore walls of the clay, and this may easily be great enough to burst the brick, as all of us have observed. Even though this steam pressure is not great enough to destroy the brick, it may be sufficient to loosen the bond of clay or produce fissures along the laminations. Such brick, though they may look sound, will invariably be weak in structure and have lost the ring of the well-burnt brick. When struck with a hammer they sound "dead."

This must be kept in mind, especially with dense, plastic clays which have such fine pores that the steam can not escape rapidly, and also dry pressed brick whose particles cohere so loosely that it does not take much pressure to break the bond. Two factors must hence be kept in mind. First, the temperature must not be kept higher than 200 degrees Centigrade, and, second, ample time must be allowed for the gradual heating up of the clay, so that no more steam is formed at any one time than can safely pass off through the pores.

It must be remembered that the expulsion of the hygroscopic water from a large kiln of ware is not such a simple process as it appears. While the upper courses of bricks in a down draft kiln lose their water, the lower courses which are still cold not only do not lose any water, but actually gain some. This is due to the fact that the steam evolved from the upper courses on striking the cold bricks in the bottom of the kiln is condensed to water which is absorbed eagerly by the clay. The lower brick thus are compelled, later on, not only to give off their own hygroscopic water, but the additional, absorbed water as well, and hence more time must be given them. This is why we can not rush the process. The kiln draft also plays an important part in this connection. If there were a strong draft in the kiln the lower course would not absorb much water, as the circulation there is too rapid. Unfortunately, at this stage the draft is very sluggish, in fact often to such an extent that the bricks of the lower courses are softened by the condensed steam, so that they can not support the load and are squashed. It behooves us, then, to look after the draft, if we expect to do the watersmoking in the shortest possible time. This is realized by clayworkers, and we sometimes heat up the stack by means of a fire in a temporary furnace built close to the stack. Again, we can provide better draft in the case where the same stack is used for several kilns and one of them is in high fire while the other is watersmoking. The hot stack will induce the necessary draft. Another way is to use fan draft or to do the watersmoking by means of warm air blown in from a cooling kiln. In this way we can solve all watersmoking troubles and save much valuable time.

In regard to controlling the kiln temperature, the use of watersmoking thermometers is strongly to be advised. There are many cases, especially in making paving brick, where much harm is done in watersmoking, though this is not realized as fully as could be desired. Many paving brick have their structure weakened by too rapid expulsion of their hygroscopic water, and if more attention were paid to this point the bricks would show up better in the rattler test. The point when all of the hygroscopic water is driven off is usually determined by the time honored method of sticking a cold rod into the kiln flue. When moist on withdrawal, steam is still coming off; when dry, the watersmoking is finished. The clayworker with scientific aspirations could easily arrange a simple apparatus consisting of several so-called absorption tubes filled with phosphorous pentachloride and connected by means of rubber tubes to a large, closed, tin can holding, say, three gallons of water. By attaching the other end of the absorption appartus to a pipe which enters into the kiln flue and allowing the water to run slowly out of the can a volume of air coming from the kiln equal to the volume of three gallons of water is drawn through the absorption tube. The phosphorous pentachloride eagerly takes up all of the water vapor in the air. The absorption tubes are weighed before and after the experiment, and if any water vapor from the ware is still in the flue gas, this is indicated by the difference in weight observed. A small balance reading to 0.01 gram can be purchased for a few dollars and would be suitable for this purpose. Such a procedure is, of course, unnecessary in practical work, but it has been suggested as showing that there is an accurate way of getting at the matter.

CHAPTER III.

Dehydration and Oxidation.

IN THE LAST article we discussed the complete drying or watersmoking of the ware. We are now ready to raise the heat and proceed to the next stages of the burning, dehydration and oxidation. The primary object after expelling the hygroscopic water must be the expulsion of other volatile matter contained in the clay, namely, the chemical water, the carbonic acid of the carbonates, the sulphur, and finally we must get rid of the carbon which would, as we have learned, cause us trouble by continuing to burn all through the balance of the process. These two functions must be kept in mind, decomposition of the clay substance and carbonates, and oxidation of the carbon, the sulphides and the ferrous iron.

Decomposition requires the expenditure of heat, oxidation gives out heat. In order to carry on the former, nothing but a sufficiently high temperature is required, while for the latter the temperature must be high enough to start combustion and at the same time sufficient air must be introduced to cause the carbon to burn. In the nature of the case these two processes overlap each other and are carried on simultaneously, although as a rule the chemical water and the carbonic acid are expelled before all of the carbon is burnt out. In this connection it also becomes important to ask how fast this can be done, for it is evident that for reasons of economy we are desirous of doing this as rapidly as possible.

The expulsion of the chemical water and of the carbonic acid usually can be carried on fairly rapidly unless the ware is extremely dense, owing to the fact that heat is consumed in these reactions. This may be observed quite well when we dehydrate a clay containing but little carbon. In placing a pyrometer in the kiln we will find that during this stage the temperature rises very slowly in spite of the fact that we fire considerably heavier than we did during the water-smoking. The heat we are putting into the kiln is evidently used up in releasing the chemical water and converting it into steam as well as in breaking up the carbonates. The utilization of heat in this chemical work has, hence, a tendency to keep down the temperature automatically. Yet, though this is so, we must remember that time must be given the steam and carbonic acid to escape without causing too great a pressure within the ware, especially when the latter is dense and close-grained. Plastic clays, especially in the shape of end cut brick, require more time for this purpose than do sandy clays. In the writer's observation of brick kilns he has found that in some cases shale brick were satisfactorily dehydrated in thirty-six hours, and in others in forty-eight hours after the watersmoking was finished. It is not advisable to linger longer than this in doing this work. From the standpoint of economy it is better to advance as soon as possible to the temperature at which oxidation takes place most rapidly. Just after dehydration is finished we observe that the ware is far more porous than at any other stage, and this is easily explained by the fact that the loss of the chemical water and of at least part of the carbonic acid gas is bound to result in additional pore-space. It is at this stage that a brick when soaked in water will absorb the greatest weight. Naturally, the strength of the clay at this stage is still very low, and if exposed to freezing weather it could not stand without crumbling. The color also has not yet begun to be developed, and the ordinary red burning clay shows a pale pinkish shade.

The progress of dehydration could best be followed by removing a brick from the kiln from time to time, weighing and replacing it. We would note a decrease in weight as long as any chemical water remained in the brick. Therefore, as soon as the brick would no longer lose water the dehydration could be considered as having been completed, provided, of course, that the kiln temperature is sufficiently high, not lower than 650 C., which is the proper practical dehydration temperature. It has even been suggested to attach a heavy piece of the ware to a stout wire carried out through the arch of the kiln and attached to one end of a counter-balanced beam. At the other end of the beam a scale pan is to be connected, so that the piece of ware can be weighed without taking it out of the kiln. In this manner an excellent record of the dehydration process could be obtained and we would know exactly when this process is finished. If, at the same time, pyrometer readings were taken we could establish the proper rate of dehydration with accuracy, and subsequently, of course, the experiment would not need to be repeated. It is this kind of simple and practical experimenting which lends interest to the prosaic subjects of clayworking and at the same time replaces the old rule of thumb methods by accurate knowledge. One does not need to be a college graduate to do this kind of work and a modicum of common sense is all that is required.

The decomposition of the carbonates stretches over a longer period and since, with the exception of limey clays, the amount of carbonic acid in clays is not very great, this part is not followed so readily and is also not of such great importance. Just as soon as the carbonate of lime has been decomposed, leaving caustic lime, the reaction between the lime and the clay begins, a reaction not tending to immediate fusion, but one involving the union of some of the silica with the lime that is forming a silicate of lime and probably also of alumina. In other words, the lime is getting ready for its final fluxing effect, though showing no signs of fusion. It is rather a kind of dry chemical consolidation, if one might use this term. Parallel with the decomposition of the carbonate of lime the ferrous carbonate loses its carbonic acid, leaving the iron as ferrous oxide, which, however, in the presence of the large volume of air (oxygen), is being oxidized to ferric oxide, providing there is but little carbon in the clay. If it contains much carbon the oxygen will be used to oxidize the latter and the iron will remain in the ferrous state.

The chemical water having been gotten rid of we can now proceed to the oxidation stage proper. It must be clearly realized, however, that there is no sharp division line between dehydration and oxidation, but that oxidation is taking place to some extent parallel with dehydration. If it were not that the carbon must be burnt out of the clay and all the iron changed to ferric oxide, we could at once proceed to the vitrification stage and would not be compelled to spend time and fuel for this purpose. But this can not be helped; we are compelled to oxidize. There are two main questions to be answered in this respect: First, what is the best temperature for oxidation? Second, how much time must we devote to it? In answering them there are involved several self-evident propositions. Up to a certain limitation we can say that the higher the temperature the more rapidly will the carbon be eliminated, just as a hot fire burns more coal per minute than a smoldering one. The more air, that is, oxygen, we pass through the kiln the more carbon will be burnt, for without oxygen there can be no combustion. We can not expect to do much burning if we fill the kiln with the combustion gases, that is, carbonic acid gas. In fire extinguishers we produce this gas for the purpose of stopping combustion. Again, the longer we burn the more carbon is naturally consumed. The length of time necessary for oxidation thus depends upon the amount and kind of carbon in the clay, the temperature, the amount of air passing through the kiln, and the size and the density of the ware.

Surface clay contains on the average about 0.5 per cent. of carbon, usually in the form of organic matter which burns out readily; fire clay contains perhaps 1 per cent., and shales from no carbon to as high as 10 per cent. More than this amount causes the shale to be unworkable. Many shales containing about 5 per cent. can be worked, but cause constant trouble and increase the cost of manufacture considerably. The quantity and kind of carbon obviously is of great importance, as naturally we should expect to find greater difficulty in burning out 6 per cent. of carbon than 1 per cent. The kind of carbon is likewise of particular significance with regard to the temperature of oxidation. If the clay contains bituminous carbon oxidation must proceed at a far lower temperature than when the carbon is similar to anthracite. If a bituminous clay is burnt at too high temperature we have not only the burning of the hydrocarbons to consider, but also their distillation, for the higher the temperature the more of these hydrocarbons will be evolved and the large volume of gas will result in a pressure which weakens or bursts the structure of the ware. At the same time, naturally, the gas distilled off will flash into flame and raise the heat very rapidly, so that the temperature will reach the vitrification or even fusion point, in which case the ware is ruined. Where the hydrocarbons are very high it is advisable to stop firing entirely for some time, the heat of the kiln being kept up by the burning of the carbon and the clay and, in some places, it is even necessary to close up the kiln tight in order that the combustion may proceed slow enough and do no harm. A case of this kind has been mentioned in the second report of the N. B. M. A. committee on technical investigation, in which 88 hours were required to remove the carbon. That the use of such a clay will materially lessen the annual capacity of a kiln is self-evident. In another instance the oxidation of paving brick from bituminous shale required seven days.

As to the best temperature for carrying on oxidation most efficiently Orton and Griffin have found that 800° C. is the most economical heat to carry, as it involves the expenditure of the least amount of time. The writer favors a somewhat lower temperature, about 750° C.

In regard to the amount of air in the fire gases the statement can be made that the more air they contain the more rapidly will oxidation proceed. It has been shown that a certain clay, when oxidized under ordinary conditions by the fire gases and admixed air required 88 hours, while only 30 hours were needed when the brick were kept surrounded by pure air in a muffle. Though the conditions of a muffle kiln can not be produced in a brick kiln, yet the fact remains that we can imitate them to a certain extent and this is done by allowing the kiln to cool down from, say, 800° to 650° C., during which time no firing is done. The place of the fire gases is then taken by the pure air and oxidation will proceed far more rapidly than it would if a steady stream of fire gases were allowed to pass through the kiln. The fires are then started again, and the heat is pushed up to the starting point, and the procedure repeated.

The density and size of the ware obviously influences greatly the rate at which oxidation must take place. While a soft mud brick can be readily oxidized, owing to its great porosity, which allows air to penetrate into the interior, this is not true of the stiff mud product, especially if made by the end-cut process. Much more time is required and the oxidation must proceed far more slowly. Similarly, dry pressed brick are also oxidized more easily than stiff mud brick, but not as readily as the soft mud.

The question as to the temperature and the kiln conditions has been sufficiently answered. There remains only to determine how long oxidation must proceed. This must be worked out for each clay and, fortunately, it is a very easy matter. By cutting a number of green brick into halves and arranging them in the kiln in a row, close to the door, so that they can be drawn out readily by means of a hook, at intervals of six or twelve hours, we have a means of telling exactly when the process of oxidation is finished. As long as there is some carbon left in the clay there will be found, on breaking the half brick, a dark or black spot in the middle which disappears only after all of the carbon has burnt out. This, hence, furnishes an absolute means of determining the finishing point of oxidation, which is as simple and practical as anything can be. The progress of oxidation can be traced down by observing the decrease in the sizes of the dark spots which gradually become smaller and smaller.

The penalty for not carrying oxidation to its finish has already been discussed. As long as there is carbon left in the clay the iron will remain in the ferrous state. This means that as soon as the temperature is high enough it will combine with the silica to form ferrous silicate, which vitrifies or fuses suddenly, thus enclosing that portion of the brick still containing carbon. Any carbonic acid or carbon monoxide forming will cause a pressure which bloats the brick or at least causes the structure of the clay to become vesicular and weak. This formation of ferrous silicate takes place, it must be remembered, far below the proper vitrification temperature, where the iron is present as ferric oxide.

CHAPTER IV.

Vitrification.

AFTER THE OXIDATION process is completed the temperature of the kiln can now be raised, and the burning may proceed more rapidly towards the finish. In this part of the burn the changes wrought by the heat upon the clay are more pronounced and more evident to the eye. If oxidation has been carried on at about 800 C., the clay will be found to possess some strength, decidedly greater than that at dehydration. As the temperature is raised the strength increases quite rapidly, although the structure may continue to appear the same. What causes this change in hardness? Evidently the first stage of vitrification is being entered upon. We may say, therefore, that vitrification extends over a long range of temperature, and is at work long before the familiar earmarks of the typical vitrified body are observed. As the name implies, vitrification is a process tending to form glass, that is, to fuse the clay into glass. Now, this fusion begins, we might say, during and immediately after oxidation, resulting first in the consolidation and hardening of the clay. That we observe at first no evidence of vitrification is due to the fact that the amount of fusible matter in the clay at the low temperature in question is very small. It just suffices to bring about some cementing action, but no more. On raising the temperature just a little higher, more of the fusible matter is formed and the clay becomes more compact; at still a higher temperature the quantity of fusible material is again larger, and we may be able to observe the change by the glassy or vitrified appearance of the clay body. This continues until complete vitrification, and finally fusion, has taken place.

The rate of vitrification depends primarily upon the character and the amount of fusible material present. By fusible material we mean that combination of silica, alumina, iron oxide, lime and alkalies present in the clay, which will produce the most fusible mixture possible. This most fusible combination necessarily differs for every clay. A fire clay evidently contains not only a smaller amount of this low fusing mixture, but also the latter differs in its composition from the most fusible combination of a paving brick shale or a lime carrying glacial material. According to natural laws the first fused portion of a clay, small though it be in amount, always represents the lowest melting combination it is possible to produce. The composition of the fluxing aggregate varies likewise as the temperature rises. The fluxing portion of the same clay at 900° differs decidedly from the one at 1,000°; it not only is greater in amount, but also is composed of a different combination of silica, alumina, iron, lime and alkalies, being richer in silica, and when taken by itself, naturally more infusible than the mixture at the lower temperature. This variable flux is called eutectic combination by the theoretical investigators. As the amount of fused matter increases in a clay it creeps through the interstices between the coarser grains of clay and finally surrounds them, at the same time filling up the pores. Thus the apparent volume of the ware decreases, and we have what is called fire shrinkage.

The first fluxing combination probably involves the fine grained feldspar, iron oxide and lime; later, as the temperature rises the fine portion of the quartz is drawn into solution, then, perhaps, more of the above fluxes, the coarser feldspar grains being gradually attacked until finally only the coarser quartz particles retain their shape, being surrounded on all sides by a fused magma. In other words, the whole process is a kind of a solution.

In the nature of the case, the glass forming reactions are never allowed to be complete, as we do not care to soften the body too much. Enough of a firm skeleton must remain to hold up the structure.

It is evident from this, hence that the physical structure, and especially the size of grain of the different minerals present, is of vital importance in governing the kind and amount of the body flux to be formed. The finer the quartz grains, for instance, the more readily they will be dissolved and assimilated, and vice versa. This is the reason why we sometimes add sand or coarse grog in order to assist the body in retaining its shape. It is needless to repeat that the many variations in the vitrification of different clays are, in a large measure, caused by differences in fineness of grain.

As to the rapidity of fusion, the presence of lime and ferrous oxide is, as we know, of decided significance. Any lime content above, say, 7 per cent. of lime, will hasten vitrification so that such a clay may be useless for purposes like the manufacture of paving brick. In all clay wares the interval between the point of complete vitrification and the point of fusion should be as large as possible, since, evidently, this means safe burning. In the case of the presence of ferrous oxide we have obviously only one remedy, complete oxidation before attempting to raise the heat.

For the purpose of considering the various stages of the process, taking the clay through vitrification to fusion, we can divide it into several steps, depending on what kind of a fracture the clay shows, and the amount of water absorbed by it. Thus we have the stony or earthen fracture stage, incipient, dense, complete and viscous vitrification, and finally fusion.

The first stage is the one commonly found in common building brick. No sign of glassiness is shown, the clay absorbs water eagerly and in considerable amounts; the color is a light red, and the iron is, to a large extent, present as the uncombined ferric oxide. Incipient vitrification is indicated by the darker color, and especially by the fact that the clay absorbs much less water and also takes up the latter more slowly. For a certain clay which the writer has in mind the water absorbed during the earthy stage was about 15 per cent., and during the incipient vitrification stage about 7 per cent. The hardness as expressed by the crushing strength is considerably greater also, being approximately 8,000 pounds per square inch compared with 4,500 pounds for the earthy stage, the clays being worked by the stiff mud process in each case. Neither of the two degrees of burning, of course, allow the brick to be used for paving purposes.

In the dense vitrification stage we observe that the pores are largely closed, and that the absorption of water is reduced to about 1 per cent. of the weight of the clay. The color is darkened to a chocolate brown, and for many paving brick clays the maximum toughness is displayed. We might say, therefore, that the clay is at its best at this point. The fracture shows a dense, compact, but not a glassy surface In complete vitrification we have practically no absorption of water, the color is darkened still more, and the fracture shows a decidedly glassy appearance. Many clays suffer a decrease in toughness though the crushing strength may be very high. The rattler test thus may bring out sharply the difference between the two stages.

In viscous vitrification the glass producing process has progressed still further, so far, in fact, that the brick are deformed and become kiln marked more or less. At the same time it is observed that the clay becomes vesicular, that is, filled with small cavities or bubbles, which cause it to become weaker and useless for paving brick. Fusion naturally is the last step, which, in our work, of course, is only accidental.

In working a clay it is, hence, important that we become acquainted with the range of the different stages, and in order to obtain this information we could proceed as follows: Make a number of brick from the same bar of clay, being careful that the bar be composed of clay of the same temper. Let these brick be marked and dried. When dry they are to be put in a position in the kiln so that they can be drawn out through the door by means of a hook. The brick might be provided with a hole for this purpose. As close to the brick as possible set a number of cones, assorted according to the nature of the clay, whether it be a red burning or a number two fire clay. In the former case use, say, eight cones—numbers 09, 07, 05, 03, 02, 1, 2, and 3; corresponding to these place in position eight or sixteen of the selected trial brick. As soon as cone 09 goes down brick No. 1 is pulled, and the same thing is done for the other cones, the firing, of course, to proceed as usual. These brick, as soon as drawn, should be covered heavily with dry, hot sand, so as to cool them as slowly as possible. When cooled, each brick is to be weighed, and then allowed to soak in water for 48 hours. Still better, the brick might be boiled in water and then soaked for the time specified. This process helps along the expulsion of air from the pores of the clay. By weighing the brick again the weight of water absorbed by each is ascertained. Dividing the weight of water absorbed by each brick by the weight of the brick, and multiplying by one hundred, we obtain the per cent of water absorption. This enables us to compare the porosities, and to judge the progress of vitrification. Naturally, the brick farthest from vitrification will absorb the most water, while the vitrified trial shows little or no absorption. If the decrease in the amount of water absorbed is a gradual one, extending over a number of cones, the vitrification is gradual, which shows that the clay has a safe range. This enables us to pick out the standard amount of water absorption, which our best brick should have.

Supposing, then, if we are making paving brick, we go into a kiln just being emptied and pick out a lot of brick from top to bottom, and allow all of them to soak, and determine the water absorbed by them. Then we classify the brick, having first marked them when dry with numerals painted on with white paint, so that, for instance, brick absorbing from no water to 1 per cent. are put in one class, those taking up from 1 to 2 per cent. into another, the 2 to

4 per cent. brick into the third, 4 to 5 per cent. into the fourth, and the 5 to 7 per cent. into the fifth. By testing each batch of the brick in the rattler, we will soon have a pretty good idea which vitrification range is best for our product.

If we care to represent our absorption results graphically, so as to obtain a picture of the progress of vitrification, we could take a sheet of ordinary co-ordinate paper, and plot the cone numbers along the bottom and the per cent. absorption along the side. The curve produced by joining the points will give us a good idea of what our clay does.

As to the water absorption test, of course. we can go as far as we please in regard to accuracy, though it would not be necessary. We could use small brick, soak them in water in a bell jar connected to a simple water suction pump which draws out the air from the pores, and permits of a more thorough absorption. In this case we would not use an ordinary grocer's scale, but would resort to the use of a little more accurate balance.

In some engineers' specifications we read statements in regard to a specific gravity requirement, and as they are put they are sheer nonsense. But it might cause us to ask whether there is any relation between the specific gravity of clay and its vitrification. In answer to this question we must acknowledge that there is, though at first sight it will puzzle us somewhat. By specific gravity of a substance we mean the ordinary weight of it, divided by its loss of weight when suspended in water. This is best illustrated by taking metric weights. Supposing we take a piece of burnt clay and find it to weigh 100 grams. We then allow it to soak in all the water it can and tie a fine silk thread around it and suspend it from the beam of a balance in a glass of water. On weighing it in this condition, we obtain as its weight 61.5 grams. It has lost, when suspended in water, 100-61.5 grams, which is equal to 38.5 grams. Now, dividing the ordinary weight in air, 100 grams, by the loss in weight, 38.5 grams, we obtain the specific gravity, which is almost 2.6. In other words, the clay is 2.6 times as heavy as water. Scientifically speaking, the specific gravity of a substance is its weight in air, divided by the volume of water displaced by it, or its own volume. In the accurate sense we call it density.

The way in which we have obtained the specific gravity of our piece of clay is not entirely accurate, as there are some air bubbles or blisters inside of the clay, which tend to make it appear lighter, and we can not fill these cavities with water, as they are closed up. Yet it does not matter very much, as we can get all the information we need from this simple determination.

To come back to our original question, we ask again, what relation is there between specific gravity and vitrification? To be brief, we can say that clay becomes lighter as vitrification proceeds. Or, in other words, a cubic inch of clay, at the "earthy" stage, weighs more than a cubic inch of vitrified or even fused clay. The writer realizes that it appears to be a paradoxical proposition, for does it not seem that the clay must become denser as it shrinks in the fire? Yet the fact remains that the farther vitrification has progressed the smaller will be its specific gravity, as any one can prove for himself by making the simple experiment. The decrease in specific gravity is due to the natural phenomenon that on partial or complete fusion of a silicate the density decreases. In addition, numerous small cavities or bubbles, which form inside of the clay, likewise tend to decrease the apparent density or specific gravity.

As early as 1828 the chemist Rose found that vitrified, translucent porcelain had a lower specific gravity than the opaque, underburnt material of the same composition. A number of other experimenters have found the same to be true.

For this reason we could determine for each temperature the specific gravity of a clay, just as we found the absorptions of water by burning at different cones. Similarly, we could also find the best specific gravity of a clay at which it shows the most desirable properties. In addition, we would obtain the vitrification range of a clay, for the quicker the specific gravity drops from cone to cone the more rapid must be the progress of vitrification, and hence the shorter the range of vitrification, that is, the less suitable the clay would be for most purposes, and vice versa. In exact clay testing, the drop in specific gravity, therefore, is a matter to which attention must be paid.

CHAPTER V.

Coloration.

THERE REMAINS yet to discuss the changes brought about by heat upon the surfaces of clay ware. The color shown by clay ware after burning depends upon the composition of the clay and the character of the firing conditions. Seger divides for this purpose the clays into the following groups:

1. Clays high in iron oxide, low in alumina, and free from lime. Red burning in oxidizing gases.

2. Clays high in iron oxide and lime, but low in alumina. Buff burning.

3. Clays fairly high in alumina and with a moderate iron oxide content, about three per cent. of the latter. Buff burning.

4. Clays high in alumina and low in iron. White to light buff burning.

1. The first class is represented by the usual red burning clay in which the iron oxide varies from about five to nine per cent., and the alumina from about ten to twenty-two per cent. These clays burn to all shades of red in oxidizing conditions, but when the gases are reducing in char-

acter the color darkens and may become gray to black. The same change takes place also under oxidizing conditions when the temperature is carried too high, though there are a few clays which retain their bright red color, even when vitrified. These, however, require very careful burning, and any reduction due to careless firing is at once shown by the dark color produced. Wherever a good red color is desired, reducing fire conditions should be strictly avoided. The presence of sulphuric acid has no particular effect on the color if oxidizing conditions prevail, its tendency is beneficial rather than otherwise, as far as color is concerned. Sulphuric acid counteracts reducing conditions and assists the clay in retaining its red color, provided oxidation follows; the red color under these conditions tends to assume a violet tint.

Red burning clays thus can easily be made to assume a dark or even black color by causing reducing conditions to prevail during the last part of the burn. That is, all we need to do is to fire heavily, causing black smoke to fill the entire kiln. According to the length of the reducing firing the black color penetrates more or less deeply into the ware. We can intensify the reduction by introducing into the kiln some hydrocarbon, like tar, crude oil, or similar cheap substance, whose vapors will penetrate into every part of the kiln. In this case, of course, the color will be an intense black. On the other hand, by facing the brick and sanding them, a less intense reduction will partially blacken the face, leaving a red colored space in the middle. This results in a pleasing effect which architects have not been slow in using. We see, therefore, that simply by regulating the firing conditions we may have red, gray or black colors obtained from the same clay. The claim made by some that a special compound is necessary to produce the black color is, of course, absurd.

In England, the bluish black Staffordshire brick, known as clinkers, and used quite extensively for pavements, and, in the shape of tiles, for floors, are produced in just this way. In other European countries, especially in Holland, this reduction is carried still farther in the manufacture of the so-called blue-smoked roofing tiles. In this case the reducing conditions caused by introducing into the kiln, wood, or especially hydrocarbons, like tar or refuse oil, are so intense that not only all of the iron is reduced to ferrous oxide, magnetic oxide or metallic iron, but some carbon in the form of graphite is actually deposited in the pores of the clay. In this manner the surface of the ware becomes coated with the silver gray graphite, which gives a color well liked by the consumers in certain districts. In some places the process of blue-smoking is carried on by firing the kiln to the proper temperature and then closing up the furnaces and all other openings and crevices air tight. After an hour or two the oil or tar is introduced into the kiln in intervals. The heat volatilizes the oil and at the same time decomposes it. Intense reduction thus takes place. The kiln is then allowed to cool and kept closed air tight. In fact, some of the manufacturers hasten the cooling by spraying water onto the kiln crown. The success of the process depends upon the cooling of the ware without the admission of air, at least not while the kiln shows red heat. If a current of air were allowed to enter the kiln the carbon would be again burnt out, and to some extent the iron would be reoxidized, thus restoring, in part at least, the lighter gray or even the red color. The same principle holds, of course, also, in the burning of the dark colored or black brick mentioned above. It is important that the kiln be cooled down to a dark red heat, closed as tight as possible. From this point on, the cooling may be hurried by exhausting air from the kiln.

2. Clays high in iron and lime, but low in alumina, carrying, say, six per cent. ferric oxide and fourteen per cent. carbonate of lime, burn, as we know, to a cream or buff color, owing to the interaction of the iron and lime which destroys the red color due to the iron. When vitrified, such a clay shows a green color and when fused it forms a brown or black slag. A clay of this character, when applied as a glaze upon such ware as stoneware, is found to be a brown and black glass, which, when cooled slowly, becomes red on the surface. The Albany slip clay belongs to this class. If a calcareous clay of this kind contains sulphates, that is, sulphuric acid, either naturally or by absorption from the kiln gases, the lime is held by the sulphuric acid and is thus prevented from reacting with the iron. Under these conditions the clay burns to a reddish color. However, by causing reducing conditions to prevail, followed by oxidation, the sulphuric acid is expelled and the union between the iron and lime takes place with the resumption of the cream color. If reduction is carried on too long and intensely, some of the ferric oxide is reduced to the ferrous state and subsequent oxidation may, at least in part, result in the production of a red color.

3. The type of clays containing a fairly large amount of alumina and moderate content of iron is represented by the so-called No. 2 fire clays, used so largely in the manu-

facture of buff and flashed front brick. In these the alumina runs from about nineteen to twenty-six per cent., the iron oxide from 1.5 to nearly three per cent. The iron nearly always is present in two forms: Some finely divided ferric oxide in the clay body itself and fine or coarser grains of iron pyrites. These clays always burn to a lighter or darker buff under oxidizing conditions except when exposed to high temperatures. In the latter case, the grains of pyrites boil out on the surface and form pimples and blotches. When burned normally these grains are not perceptible. In the manufacture of the so-called flashed brick, the No. 2 fire clays are exposed to reducing conditions, so that we have the pimples of the black slag on the surface, and, in addition, have likewise converted the small amount of finely divided ferric oxide to the ferrous oxide. If, therefore, a brick were pulled out of the kiln immediately after reduction, it would show a light or grayish background covered by the black spots. There would be no evidence whatever of any flash. Where, then, is the reddish or golden colored flash produced? Evidently in the cooling. The air entering the white hot kiln passes through the bricks and oxidizes the surface of the ware, forming that flush of reddish brown or golden color known as flash. It is evident, therefore, that the rate of cooling is bound to influence the kind of flash produced. Slow cooling must necessarily produce more flash than rapid cooling. The reduction has an effect with regard to the amount of the iron forming the black spots. The more intense the reducing effect the more of these must be brought out.

The presence of sulphuric acid in these clays, especially in the oxidizing fire, tends to give a pinkish film of color, which occasionally persists after reduction and subsequent oxidation. This frequently is very annoying to the manufacturer of front brick.

4. Clays high in alumina and low in iron are represented by the kaolins, china clays, ball clays, and No. 1 fire clays. These are rarely burnt alone, excepting the fire clays used in making fire brick where color is practically immaterial. Usually they are employed in mixtures with feldspar, flint, and perhaps a little lime in the production of porcelain, whiteware, tiles, etc. The kaolins burn nearly always to a clean white color, whether the kiln conditions be oxidizing or reducing. At higher temperatures, when burnt alone, they assume a creamish tint in the oxidizing fire, while in the reducing atmosphere they retain their white color, or, if the iron is somewhat high, a grayish tint is shown. Sulphuric acid has no effect upon these clays in the oxidizing condition, but on reduction gives rise to a pinkish surface effect. On oxidation in gases free from sulphuric acid this color disappears.

The ball and fire clays have a decided cream color after burning. In the former the iron is, as a rule, quite finely disseminated. In the latter iron pyrites occur in small amount, which, at the high temperatures of burning, cause spots of reduced iron slag to show on the surface. In bodies composed of kaolin, ball clay, and feldspar, it is advisable to close the firing with slightly reducing conditions, so as to maintain as white a color as possible. This is to be followed by cooling as rapidly as is practicable. If the kiln conditions were strongly oxidizing at the close of the burn and the cooling slow, the ware would assume a cream color, due to the ferric oxide, which would render the ware unsalable.

CHAPTER VI.

Artificial Brick Colors.

WE CAN NOT CLOSE this series of articles without referring briefly to the colors which we may produce in the body or on the surface of our clay wares by artificial means. The use of coloring compounds within the clay bodies is necessarily limited by the cost of the available substances and excepting for such ware as floor and wall tiles and some classes of terra cotta we are practically restricted to the use of iron oxide and manganese oxide (pyrolusite). Finely ground iron ore may, in some cases, be used as a help in obtaining darker colors, but as a rule the results are not as satisfactory as they might be on account of the difficulty of incorporating the oxide immediately with the clay, or rather the cost of doing so. In most cases, unless special care is taken to insure uniform distribution, the color is apt to be irregular.

Wherever the color of the clay is to be improved or enriched it is always best, if possible, to use another clay very high in ferric oxide or clayey or sandy materials, like ochre. The results of such mixtures will be found more satisfactory. In some instances, as in flashed brick, the use of granular magnetic oxide may be desirable, since in this case it is not a question of uniformity of color, but of producing the dark specks necessary in flashed brick. Other iron ores, like hematite, may, of course, also be used for this purpose and an addition of two or two and one-half per cent. of such an iron compound will help to produce the dark flashed colors desired.

Manganese oxide, in several grades of fineness is used with No. 2 fire clays to produce the well known gray or speckled brick, usually made by the dry press process. The amount added varies, according to the desired shade, from one to two and one-half per cent. The finer grained oxide will, of course, produce more the effect of a solid color, while the granular kind shows the speckled effect. Two conditions are necessary to produce a good gray, and these are: First, a clay burning to a clean and very light color, which must not be too buff, so as to give a suitable background for the black oxide; second, the burning must be carried on under oxidizing conditions and at as low a temperature as will bring out the black color of the manganese. In regard to the latter it is always the best policy to use a pure grade, since more impure manganese ores will fuse too readily and will cause the formation of a black slag on the surface which will cause the brick to stick together, besides rendering them worthless so far as appearance is concerned. The best grade is usually the cheapest in the end.

In regard to surface colors we have available a somewhat larger variety of effects and colors, since the amount of the coloring material need not be so large in amount, and hence the cost for the better grades of front brick is not prohibitive. Such methods of varying the colors of brick are used more in Europe and it seems to the writer that this subject ought to be taken up more extensively by American manufacturers. We refer to the use of slips on engobes. By these we mean natural or artificial clay mixtures which are applied onto the surface of the brick made by the stiff clay process in the form of a liquid slip, or as a plastic mass. The object of their use is either to produce a more uniform color, in which case the same clay employed for the bricks themselves is purified by washing and applied, or to produce a color different from that of the body.

It is evident that the slip, whatever be its purpose, must have the same drying and burning shrinkage as the body and must adhere perfectly, burning to a dense surface. There are many clays which, by the addition of perhaps a little fluxing material like Cornwall stone and a very small amount of lime, would be excellent slip clays. The case is simplest, of course, where the same clay from which the ware is made is used as an engobe. This may be practiced where the unwashed clay is not of a satisfactory color and the washed and screened material will produce a uniform and better color effect. In such a case it would probably be still better to use a richer colored natural clay for the slip entirely, which is frequently done in Europe.

If a color like green is desired for a serpentine-like effect in which the coloring substance is chrome oxide, it is evident that the slip clay, besides possessing the necessary shrinkage qualification and burning to a dense layer, must be very light in color, in fact, as white as possible, so as to bring out the maximum coloring effect of the chrome oxide. The green color also is not brought unless the slip is practically vitrified by the addition of Cornwall stone or feldspar and a very small amount of carbonate of lime. This means that this color is not available for red burning clays, but is restricted to the No. 2 fire clays.

The chrome oxide may be prepared and incorporated in the slip mixture by three methods:

1. Some of the clay, Cornwall stone and lime carbonate and all of the chrome oxide are ground together thoroughly in the wet ball mill and calcined in the kiln, the amount of this calcine corresponding to about fifteen per cent. of the whole slip. This burnt product is then crushed and ground together with the balance of the slip constituents.

2. The chrome is added to about thirty per cent. of the slip in a blunger in the form of a soluble compound, like chromium sulphate. By adding ammonia water or carbonate of soda the chromium is precipitated in the form of a fine gelatinous mass intimately blended with the rest of the constituents. After thorough stirring, this slip is pumped into a filter press in which the water is removed and the slip left in the form of a cake. This plastic mass is then cut up and blunged in another blunger with the balance of the slip.

3. The chrome oxide may be at once added to the slip and ground thoroughly with the latter in the wet ball mill. Methods one and two are to be preferred to the third inasmuch as they will result in a far more intimate mixture and better color. All of this work is best done by a man familiar with this work or understanding the chemical principles involved. What has been said of the preparation of the chrome oxide green applies also to the other colors, though the preparation need not be so thorough in the case

of the manganese, provided the latter is ground extremely fine. The colors which may be produced in this way on No. 2 fire clays are: White, gray, black, red, buff, yellow, brown, green, and blue, and, of course, many shades obtained by blending these colors or diluting them, with white as the base.

White is produced, as has been indicated before, by a mixture of one or two white burning clays, a kaolin and a plastic light burning clay, Cornwall stone, feldspar, flint, and a small amount of whiting. At about cone 4-5 a good vitrified layer should be produced.

Gray is obtained with pulp manganese in different percentages up to three per cent. Black is prepared from a mixture of manganese and iron oxide and a very small amount of cobalt oxide. For red preferably a clean burning red clay should be employed. Buff and yellow are obtained either from a natural clay, such as is found near Sparta, Ohio, or from an artificial mixture of flint, Cornwall stone and ferric hydroxide, which are blunged together thoroughly, calcined in the kiln, and the calcine ground intimately with the balance of the slip. In some cases, if ferric chloride is used, the iron hydroxide may be precipitated with ammonia right in the slip and after blunging the slip may be used without the necessity of calcining the iron.

Brown is produced by intimate blending of a red burning clay with manganese and chrome oxide. Green, as has been described before, is due to chrome oxide. Blue, which is prepared similarly to the chromium color, is obtained from cobalt oxide, from one-half to two per cent. being sufficient for this purpose.

The application of the slips may be accomplished by hand-dipping, mechanical covering, or by spraying. The first method is the most expensive and unsatisfactory one. Mechanical means of applying the slips can undoubtedly be employed as the column of clay leaves the die of the auger machine, and there are several European patents covering such procedures. The problem should not be a difficult one, the main requirements being a reservoir containing the slip which is to be kept agitated and poured over the surface of the column and some kind of a polished slicker for more uniform distribution of the engobe.

Spraying by compressed air may be employed either at the machine or later when the brick are transferred to pallets.

The application of a plastic engobe outside of the die upon a clay bar is used successfully in one instance in the United States, and the method is covered by letters patent. This would seem a most satisfactory means of accomplishing the purpose of engobing, especially as it would enable the manufacturer to apply a thicker layer.

In manufacturing products of this kind repressing is not advisable, and hence the cutting tables would have to be constructed with special care, so as to produce brick exact in shape and free from rough edges. This can be done, as is successfully demonstrated by European practice. Such exact working tables using thin wires can be produced by our machine manufacturers as soon as a demand exists for them. In burning engobed brick, care would have to be taken to burn with oxidizing conditions, and clean, white sand would be necessary for sanding them in setting.

Certain color effects may be obtained also by the use of colored sands applied upon the clay column on issuing from the die, a method which is used successfully in several plants. After the sand is distributed over the surface, it is gently pressed into the clay by means of a roller.

The great claim which can be made for structural clay ware is its adaptability in regard to shape and its broad range of color. As the demands of the architects broaden it must be the aim of the clay ware manufacturer to satisfy his requirements, and, in fact, to suggest further possibilities for the outside and inside decoration of our structures, and at the same time keeping within the limits of artistic taste.

Finally, we will give brief consideration to another means of surface coloration, salt glazing, which has found some application in the manufacture of face brick. As is generally known, the glaze is produced by throwing salt into the fire boxes when the temperature has reached the maturing point, that is, near the end of the burn. The best results in salt glazing are never obtained below 1,100 C. The salt thus charged into the kiln through the fire boxes, or sometimes through the crown holes, is at once decomposed by the heat into soda and hydrochloric acid gas. The former unites with the clay to form a glass, the latter escapes from the kiln as vapor. Although in this process heat is consumed, if the fires have cleaned before salting, no trouble is experienced in maintaining the required temperature during salting. In fact, the writer has observed in one instance a rise of five degrees while the salt was being introduced. The great variety of colors that are obtained are in part due to the conditions prevailing in the kiln. When the gases are reducing in character the glaze becomes usually darker than when oxidizing conditions prevail. However, it seems to be general practice to clear the fires before salting. This also has a tendency to prevent pimpling, that is, the formation of blisters or rough spots on the surface. A better salt glaze is always produced on a ware for which the clay has been screened rather fine, and it appears that a great deal of the trouble in salt glazing is due to coarse screening. It hardly need be mentioned that the heat must not be raised too rapidly, although in the burning of sewerpipe there seems to be an inclination that way.